Contents

Words printed in **bold** can be found in the glossary.

What is a stable structure?

A stable structure is something that has been built to stand up without wobbling or falling over.

All of the buildings around us are stable structures. Houses, schools, office blocks, shops and factories need to be extremely stable to keep all the people in and around them safe.

Lots of everyday objects are stable structures, too. Tables and chairs are stable. They are built to hold heavy objects without collapsing. Music stands are made to hold sheets of music steady and in a suitable position for musicians. Slides and swings in playgrounds have to be stable so that they don't fall over when we use them.

Swings need to be very stable so that when you swing high and fast, the frame stays firmly on the ground.

The CN Tower in Toronto, Canada is the the tallest free-standing structure in the world. It is over 553 metres tall!

Stable Structures

LYNN HUGGINS-COOPER

A & C Black • London

Published 2007 by A & C Black Publishers Limited
38 Soho Square, London W1D 3HB
www.acblack.com

Hardback ISBN: 978-0-7136-7114-8
Paperback ISBN: 978-0-7136-7688-4

Editor: Sarah Gay
Designer: Miranda Snow

The author and publishers would like to thank Clare Benson and Sue Dutson for their advice in producing this series of books.

A CIP catalogue record for this book is available from the British Library.

This book is produced using paper that is made from wood grown in managed, sustainable forests. It is natural, renewable and recyclable. The logging and manufacturing processes conform to the environmental regulations of the country of origin.

Printed and bound in Singapore by Tien Wah Press (PTE) Limited.

Picture credits: front cover(br), Bryan Busovicki/Shutterstock; front cover(bl), W H Chow/Shutterstock; back cover, Florin Cirstoc/Shutterstock; 4, 21(br), geogphotos/Alamy; 5, Rudy Sulgan/Corbis; 6, Mark Karrass/Corbis; 7, Alan Copson/JAI/Corbis; 8(l), Abode/Beateworks/Corbis; 8(r), Comstock/Corbis; 9(t), Jose Fuste Raga/Corbis; 9(bl), Blaine Harrington III/Corbis; 9(br), Liba Taylor/Corbis; 10, Rob Howard/Corbis; 11, Yang Liu/Corbis; 12, Johner/Getty; 13, 25(m) Joseph Sohm/Visions of America/Corbis; 14, Carl & Ann Purcell/Corbis; 15, Robert Holmes/Corbis; 16, 22, 23(l), 23(m), 23(r), 24(m), 25(b), J Bishop/S Gay; 17, Simon Jarratt/Corbis; 18, Pinto/zefa/Corbis; 19, Yang Liu/Corbis; 20(tl), Martin Paquin/Alamy; 20(bl), Steve Chenn/Corbis; 20(br), Nick Hawkes/Ecoscene/Corbis; 21(t), Hugh Threlfall/Alamy; 21(bl), Cephas Picture Library/Alamy.

Stable structures in history

Spectacular stable structures have been built throughout history. Many of them are so stable that they are still standing for us to see today!

The **Ancient Egyptians** built enormous pyramids as tombs for the **pharaohs**. **Architects** today are still baffled by how the pyramids were built before cranes and heavy building machinery had been invented.

The **Ancient Romans** used big stone pillars to help support their buildings. They also used stone to build bridges and **aqueducts**. Today, **concrete** is often used instead because it can be moulded into shape rather than cut like stone. Concrete is much cheaper than stone, but it is nearly as strong.

◀ The Great Pyramid of Khufu was the tallest building in the world for 4000 years.

This Roman aqueduct is in the city of Segovia, Spain. ▶

Stable structures everywhere!

Stable structures, big and small, are all around us. Have a look around you. How many can you see?

▲ Bunkbeds need to take the weight of two people without collapsing.

▲ Bookshelves have to be stable enough to hold hundreds of heavy books.

The O2 is a huge structure that was built to celebrate the year 2000. It used to be called the Millennium Dome.

These houses are held up above the water by stilts.

A climbing frame has to be very sturdy so that children can climb all over it safely.

Strong materials

An important part of what makes a structure stable is the material it is made from. Some materials have certain properties which make them good for building stable structures.

Wood is cheap and quite strong. It is used for building structures such as bridges, houses, and even roller coasters! However, it rots, it can swell when wet and it burns easily. Many homes are made of stone or bricks instead, as these last longer and are not a **fire hazard**.

Plastic is light and can be moulded into different shapes. It is long-lasting, and can be quite strong. It is sometimes used to make roofs for sports arenas, and is often used for small stable structures like chairs.

Metal can also be moulded, but is much stronger and heavier than plastic. Steel and iron are types of metal often used for building because they are very sturdy. Metal can be used to **reinforce** structures made from other materials.

Tents are made with hollow metal poles and strong, waterproof fabric so they don't collapse in bad weather but are light to carry.

Try it out!

LOOK AT STRUCTURES IN YOUR LOCAL AREA

1 What are they made from? Which is the most common material?

When metal is heated to a very high temperature it becomes a glowing liquid which can be poured into moulds.

2 Are different materials used for newly built structures than for old historic buildings? If so, can you think of reasons why this might be the case?

Sketch some of the stable structures in your local area. Label the things that you think help to make them stable and strong.

Stability in width

The base of a stable structure is usually very wide. This spreads the weight of the structure over a larger area and makes it less likely to collapse or topple over!

A good example of this is a bridge. A bridge is usually built in an arch shape, so its two 'feet' are far apart from each other. This gives it a wide base which makes it stable and able to carry the weight of the structure, and the people and vehicles that cross it, without collapsing.

The frame of a playground swing has legs which are far apart.

This gives it a broad base which holds it steady in the ground while people swing high up into the air.

Some shapes are more stable than others. **Cuboids**, arches, pyramids, domes and triangles are all used to design stable structures because they have wide bases.

Ferris wheels have legs which stretch very wide to keep the wheel stable. ▶

◀ The Eiffel Tower in Paris, France is one of the most famous structures in the world. Can you see how its legs are stretched out wide to make it stable?

Triangles

The triangle is one of the most important shapes in engineering because it is so strong. A triangular structure keeps its shape and will not change however hard it is forced.

FACT!

Spaceship Earth at Disney's Epcot Centre in Florida is a huge dome made from 11,324 triangles. Each triangle is made from layers of aluminium and plastic.

The shape of a triangle is determined by the lengths of its three sides. If you change the length of one of the sides or the size of one of the angles (corners), you have to change the other sides and angles to make it a triangle again. So a triangle shape is **rigid** unless one of its sides or one of its joints is broken.

Bridges, construction cranes and buildings are often made up of triangles. Sometimes rectangles or squares are strengthened by adding a diagonal, which makes the shape into two triangles.

Many structures, like music stands and some stools, have three legs, which make their bases triangular. Three-legged structures are thought of as more stable than four-legged structures as they don't wobble even if one leg is shorter than the others.

Spaceship Earth looks like a huge golf ball. It is made up of thousands of small triangles.

Try it out!

HOW STRONG IS A TRIANGLE?

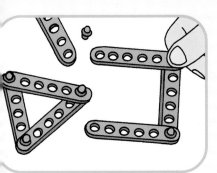 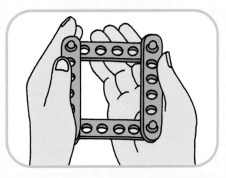 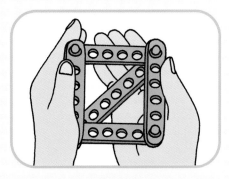

1 Use a construction kit to make a square and a triangle.

2 Experiment with the two shapes. How easy is it to change the shapes by pushing them with your hands?

3 Can you build any other strong shapes?

This bridge in San Francisco, USA, has been strengthened to withstand powerful earthquakes. Can you see all the triangle shapes in the bridge?

Strengthening structures

Sometimes we need to make materials stronger so that the structures we build are more stable. There are lots of ways of making materials stronger.

Materials can be folded or layered to make them stiffer. Plywood is very rigid and hard to break because it is made from at least three different layers of wood.

Materials such as metal, plastic and paper can be rolled or moulded into tubes. Tubes can support more weight than single sheets of material. They are hollow so they are light as well as strong. Tubes are used for chair and table legs and to support structures such as staircases.

Corrugating a material makes it much stronger. Material is corrugated by bending it into arches or zigzags, like a paper fan. The bent sheet is often glued between two flat sheets of the same material. Paper, cardboard, metal and plastic can all be corrugated.

◀ Most cardboard boxes are made out of corrugated cardboard to make them stronger. If you look carefully you can see the arches of cardboard between the two flat sheets.

Try it out!

MAKE A PAPER TABLE
You will need: newspapers, PVA glue and masking tape

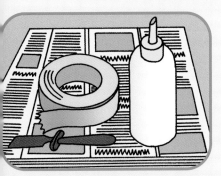  

1 Try to make a table that will support the weight of a small book, using only newspaper, PVA glue and masking tape.

2 Experiment with different **methods** to make your paper stronger. You could even try covering the paper in tape or PVA glue to make it stiffer.

3 Then put the book on your table and test it out! Does it hold the book or do you need to improve your design?

These desks and chairs all have metal tubes for legs. They can hold a lot of weight but are light so can be easily moved around, stored or stacked. ▶

Joining methods

When building a stable structure, it is important to think about how all the component parts will be joined together. The joins must be reliable and safe. Joins can add to the stability and sometimes even the strength of a structure.

When you are making a model, there are lots of ways to join the different parts. A cardboard model may have the joins held together with masking tape, sticky tape, or a paper **hinge** that is glued onto the two parts to be joined. All of these ways of joining parts help to reinforce the joint and make it stronger.

When you are joining wood, you can use glue, nails or screws.

A hinge is a joint that lets two parts of a structure move. Metal hinges are used to allow doors to open and close.

Try it out!

MAKE A BED WITH A HEADBOARD FOR A SOFT TOY

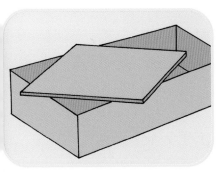  

1 Use a rectangular box for the bed and a small piece of card for the headboard. Think about how you could join the headboard to the bed.

2 When you have decided how you are going to join the headboard to your bed, go ahead and make it. Decorate it so it looks like a real bed.

3 **Evaluate** your joining method. Is your headboard stable or might it fall on the toy in the night? Can you think of any ways of joining that might work better?

Two pieces of metal can be joined together by welding. The metal is heated to a very high temperature until it begins to melt and then the pieces are joined together. When the metal cools and hardens it forms a very strong joint.

Free-standing structures

Free-standing structures are structures which stand up on their own, without leaning on or being supported by anything else. They might be made from stiff materials or have wide bases. Poles, legs or struts can also help to keep them upright. What do you think makes each of these structures stable?

▲ A stool

▼ A goal

▲ A litter bin

A garden shed

A music stand

A mug

Free-standing photo frames

Photo frames are used to display photographs and to decorate rooms. They are usually made from strong, rigid materials such as wood, metal, glass or ceramics to hold the photograph securely. Most have a transparent layer that protects the photograph from damage.

Some photo frames are made to hang on the wall, but many others are made to stand up on desks and shelves. They are made from stiff materials and may have supports such as **dowels** or **struts** attached to the back to make them stand up. Some frames are made using stable shapes which stand upright on their own.

Photo frames can be decorated and **personalised** in lots of different ways and they make great gifts.

◀ Most picture frames use a flap with a hinge to stand up.

22

Try it out!

MAKE A SHEET OF CARD STAND UP

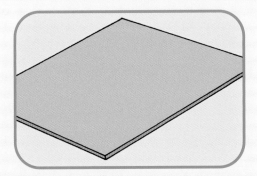

1 Find a large sheet of card. How many different ways can you find to make it stand on its edge?

2 Try experimenting with the different methods described on these two pages. Can you think of any other ways?

▲ A single block of wood has been used to make this frame, so it stands up on the wide edge of the block.

▲ This frame stands using a single piece of dowel pushed into the frame.

▲ Two frames have been joined together with a hinge, so they stand up like a birthday card.

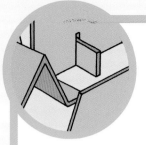

Make your own...

DESIGN AND MAKE YOUR OWN PICTURE FRAME

Design a free-standing photo frame as a gift for somebody. What sort of frame could you make? Think about who your frame is for and what kind of frame they would like. It could be made in a themed shape such as a football or a star. Sketch some designs and choose your favourite.

Think about what materials you will use to make your frame. You will need to be able to cut or shape the material. How will you put your photo inside? How will your picture frame stand up?

Draw an exploded diagram of your frame and describe how it will be made. Think about how you will join the different parts together.

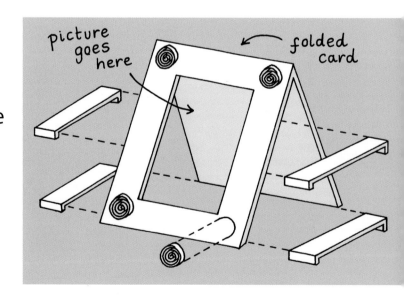

picture goes here

folded card

You may find it useful to make **prototypes** of your designs from paper – or even just the front of the frames. Ask people to give you **feedback** about the appearance of the frames. Which is the most popular? When you have got your feedback, decide which frame you are going to make.

Now make your frame carefully. Make sure you think about **quality** and presentation while you're making it. Be prepared to make adjustments to your design if you think you need to make it stronger or more stable.

When you have finished making your frame, evaluate it. Are you pleased with it? How well does it work? Does it stand up on its own? How does it compare to your original design? If you had to make it again, is there anything that you would do to improve it?

Brilliant books and wonderful websites

There are lots of great books and websites out there to help you to learn more about stable structures. When you are using the Internet, remember to be careful. Do not give out details of your age or where you live, and make sure your parents and carers have a look at the websites you are visiting. They may learn something too!

BOOKS

Skyscrapers!: Super Structures to Design and Build by Carol A. Johmann (Williamson Publishing Co, 2001)

Build It!: Structures, Systems and You By Adrienne Mason (Kids Can Press, 2006)

The Way Things Work by David Macaulay and Neil Ardley (Dorling Kindersley, 2004)

The Oxford Children's A-Z of Technology by Robin Kerrod (Oxford University Press, 2004)

Structures: Or Why Things Don't Fall Down by J.E.Gordon (Penguin, 1991)

The New Science of Strong Materials: Or Why You Don't Fall Through the Floor by J.E.Gordon (Penguin, 1991)

WEBSITES

http://www.activityvillage.co.uk/photo_frames_from_cd_boxes.htm
How to make photo frames from CD boxes

http://www.infoplease.com/ipa/A0001328.html
Stable structures around the world, from ancient to modern

http://www.tour-eiffel.fr/teiffel/uk/ludique/visite/index.html
Take a 3-D tour of the Eiffel Tower

Glossary

Ancient Egyptians	people that lived in Egypt thousands of years ago
Ancient Romans	people that were part of a huge empire that began in Rome thousands of years ago
aqueduct	a bridge that carries water from one place to another
architect	a person who designs buildings
component parts	the different parts that are put together to make something
concrete	a hard, strong building material made by mixing sand, gravel, cement and water
corrugate	to shape a material into even ridges or grooves
cuboid	a 3-D shape with six rectangular sides
dowel	a narrow wooden rod
engineering	using knowledge of science and maths to do or make practical things
evaluate	judge what you have done and decide if anything could be done better
feedback	reactions; what someone thinks about a product or process
fire hazard	something that gives a greater than normal risk of harm to people or property caused by fire
hinge	something that joins two parts together and allows one of the parts to swing open or closed
method	a way of doing something
personalise	to make something for a particular person
pharaohs	the kings of Ancient Egypt
prototype	a first version of what you are going to make, which you can improve or base your final version on
quality	how well something is made
reinforce	make something stronger or more stable
rigid	hard; not bendable
strut	a bar or rod that is used to support the weight of a structure

Index

Numbers in **bold** denote a picture.